# AMERICAN HOLIDAYS

# *Labor Day*

Lynn Hamilton

Weigl Publishers Inc.

Published by Weigl Publishers Inc.
350 5th Avenue, Suite 3304
New York, NY  USA  10118-0069
Web site: www.weigl.com

**Library of Congress Cataloging-in-Publication Data**

Hamilton, Lynn, 1964-
  Labor Day / Lynn Hamilton.
      p. cm. --  (American holidays)
Summary: Examines the history of Labor Day and describes some of the ways
that this holiday is celebrated.
Includes bibliographical references and index.
  ISBN 1-59036-129-6 (Library Bound : alk. paper) — ISBN 1-59036-166-0 (pbk.)
  1.  Labor Day--Juvenile literature. [1. Labor Day. 2. Holidays.]  I.
Title. II. American holidays (Mankato, Minn.)
  HD7791.H36 2004
  394.264--dc21
                                        2003003955

Printed in the United States of America
1 2 3 4 5 6 7 8 9 0  07 06 05 04 03

**Project Coordinator** Tina Schwartzenberger  **Substantive Editor** Heather C. Hudak
**Design** Terry Paulhus **Layout** Susan Kenyon  **Photo Researcher** Barbara Hoffman

# Contents

# Introduction

★ ★ ★ ★ ★ ★ ★ ★ ★ ★ ★ ★ ★ ★ ★ ★ ★ ★ ★ ★ ★ ★ ★ ★ ★ ★ ★ ★ ★ ★ ★

Labor Day
is a time
to recognize
the hard
work of
U.S. citizens.

## DID YOU KNOW?

Other countries
have special
holidays to
honor workers,
too. Canada
also celebrates
Labor Day on
the first Monday
in September.

Labor Day is celebrated on the first Monday in September. This holiday signals the end of summer and the start of a new school year. Families and friends gather for games, picnics, and other fun activities.

Throughout history, people have given their time and skills to help America grow and become successful. Many workers and labor leaders have struggled to gain better working conditions and rights. Labor Day is a time to recognize the hard work of U.S. citizens and labor leaders. For more than 120 years, many communities have hosted special celebrations on Labor Day.

Many people spend Labor Day with their families, often going on picnics.

# Labor and Skills

★ ★ ★ ★ ★ ★ ★ ★ ★ ★ ★ ★ ★ ★ ★ ★ ★ ★ ★ ★ ★ ★ ★ ★ ★ ★ ★ ★ ★ ★ ★ ★ ★

**Many people worked in factories, mills, and mines.**

In the 1800s, many U.S. communities needed the labor and skills of workers. **Craftspeople**, such as carpenters and tailors, made goods that people needed. Some people worked in shops. Others worked on the railroad or on farms. Many worked in factories, mills, and mines.

Some workplaces were dangerous, dusty, and noisy. Often, people who worked with machines were not safe. Many people worked 6 or 7 days each week for very low pay. Often, they worked 10 to 14 hours each day.

★ ★ ★ ★ ★

Between 1881 and 1900, there were nearly 140 **strikes** at New Jersey's Paterson Silk Plant.

## DID YOU KNOW?

Sometimes children worked to help support their families. Boys often loaded coal in mines. Girls spun thread and wool in textile mills, or factories where cloth was made.

Young women formed a large part of the labor force in the textile industry. To work in factories, many women had to move away from home and stay in boarding houses.

# Making Changes

Workers from New York State were invited to march in a parade.

## DID YOU KNOW?

In 1881, Peter J. McGuire started a carpenters' union. He also helped create the American Federation of Labor, now called the American Federation of Labor and Congress of Industrial Organizations, or AFL-CIO.

Peter J. McGuire knew the problems that many workers faced. When he was 11 years old, he quit school to work. He shone shoes and sold newspapers. As a teenager, McGuire learned a **trade** at a piano shop. He went to meetings with other workers. They talked about labor issues. Soon, McGuire was speaking to the public about workplace problems. He planned and took part in **protests**.

Matthew Maguire was a machine operator from New Jersey. He was also interested in workers' rights and belonged to labor organizations. Some people believe Matthew Maguire was the first person to suggest a celebration in honor of U.S. workers. Others believe Peter Mcguire had the idea first. The Central **Labor Union** in New York agreed with the idea. Workers from across New York State were invited to march in a parade and attend a picnic.

Peter J. McGuire worked for a Labor Day holiday in 1882. He wanted the holiday to be separate from existing holidays.

# Words of Wisdom

★ ★ ★ ★ ★ ★ ★ ★ ★ ★ ★ ★ ★ ★ ★ ★ ★ ★ ★ ★ ★ ★ ★ ★ ★ ★ ★ ★ ★ ★ ★ ★ ★ ★

Many leaders and labor **activists** have expressed their ideas about workers and Labor Day in speeches, newspaper articles, and books.

Samuel Gompers was the president of the American Federation of Labor for nearly 40 years. In 1898, he described Labor Day as a day when workers "... may not only lay down their tools of labor for a holiday, but upon which they may touch shoulders in marching... and feel the stronger for it."

★ ★ ★ ★ ★ ★ ★ ★ ★
Samuel Gompers became president of the American Federation of Labor in 1886.

# On Labor Day

On Labor Day we pay tribute to the generations of men and women who built America. We truly stand on the shoulder of giants—workers who made this country the hope of the world and the land of opportunity for millions of people.

—Elaine Chao,
Secretary of Labor

Elaine Chao has been the Secretary of Labor since January 29, 2001. She is the first Asian-American woman to hold this position.

# Creating the Holiday

★ ★ ★ ★ ★ ★ ★ ★ ★ ★ ★ ★ ★ ★ ★ ★ ★ ★ ★ ★ ★ ★ ★ ★ ★ ★ ★ ★ ★ ★ ★ ★ ★ ★

**The Central Labor Union invited other unions to hold similar events.**

On Tuesday, September 5, 1882, the first Labor Day celebrations were held in New York City. About 10,000 workers marched in the parade. They carried signs that read "Eight Hours for Work; Eight Hours for Rest; Eight Hours for Recreation!" Picnics, speeches, and fireworks followed the march.

The Central Labor Union invited other unions to hold similar events. Another celebration took place in New York the next year. Soon, many other states were celebrating the day. By 1888, Colorado, Massachusetts, New Jersey, and New York had declared Labor Day a holiday.

★ ★ ★ ★ ★ ★ ★ ★ ★

At the first Labor Day celebrations in New York City, 10,000 workers marched from City Hall to Union Square.

In 1894, workers of the Pullman Railroad Company went on strike. Union members across the United States refused to work on trains that were pulling Pullman cars. Train service across the United States stopped. President Grover Cleveland sent the army to stop the strike. Some union members were killed.

Eugene Debs was the American Railway Union leader. He was sent to prison. The strike was over, but workers were still angry. In 1894, Congress passed a law making the first Monday in September a national holiday.

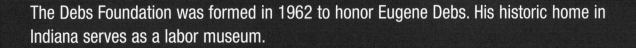

The Debs Foundation was formed in 1962 to honor Eugene Debs. His historic home in Indiana serves as a labor museum.

# Celebrating Today

★ ★ ★ ★ ★ ★ ★ ★ ★ ★ ★ ★ ★ ★ ★ ★ ★ ★ ★ ★ ★ ★ ★ ★ ★ ★ ★ ★ ★ ★ ★ ★ ★ ★

Labor Day celebrations even take place on the Internet.

The Labor Day long weekend is a time to think about the efforts of workers across the country. Many events are held on the holiday. Political leaders and labor officials make speeches about the importance of workers and about labor issues. Many communities hold parades. Festivals and fairs are often planned for the Labor Day weekend.

Labor Day is also a chance for workers to relax and spend time with their families and friends. Baseball games, golf tournaments, soccer, and tennis matches are held across the country. People also visit beaches, campgrounds, and parks. Labor Day celebrations even take place on the Internet. As part of their online Labor Day Festival, the AFL-CIO Web site offers holiday information and games.

Labor Day is considered the last long weekend of summer. Many families spend the three-day weekend camping.

# Americans Celebrate

Many Labor Day celebrations take place across the United States. This map shows just a few of these events.

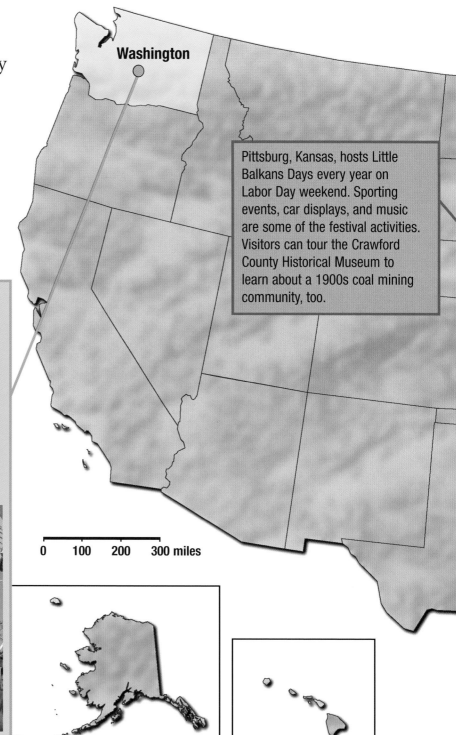

Washington

Pittsburg, Kansas, hosts Little Balkans Days every year on Labor Day weekend. Sporting events, car displays, and music are some of the festival activities. Visitors can tour the Crawford County Historical Museum to learn about a 1900s coal mining community, too.

Many county and state fairs are held on the Labor Day weekend. In Washington state, people at the Kittitas County Fair can watch a rodeo and see many farming displays. People at the Bumbershoot Festival in Seattle can enjoy the work of artists such as dancers, musicians, painters, and writers.

0    100    200    300 miles

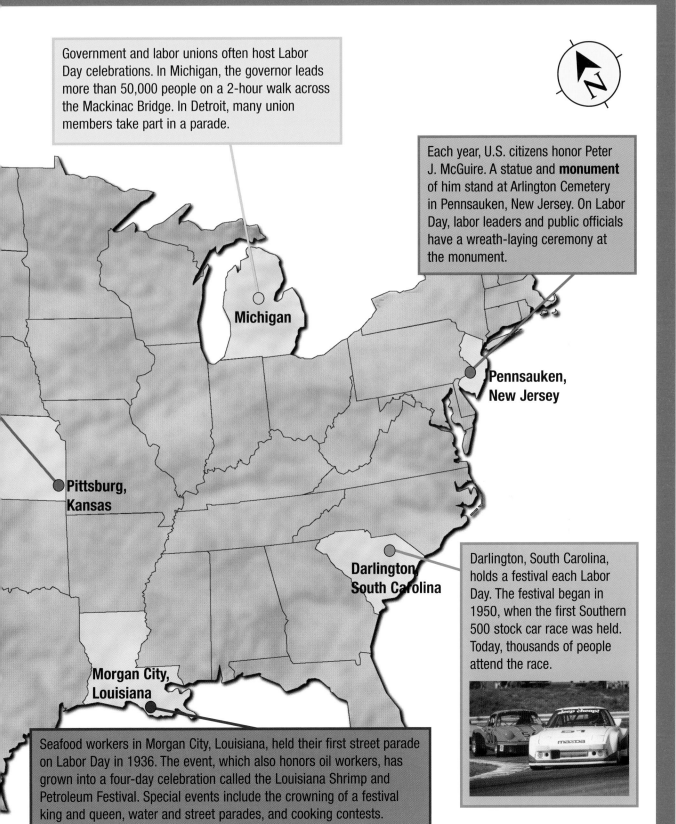

Government and labor unions often host Labor Day celebrations. In Michigan, the governor leads more than 50,000 people on a 2-hour walk across the Mackinac Bridge. In Detroit, many union members take part in a parade.

Each year, U.S. citizens honor Peter J. McGuire. A statue and **monument** of him stand at Arlington Cemetery in Pennsauken, New Jersey. On Labor Day, labor leaders and public officials have a wreath-laying ceremony at the monument.

**Michigan**

**Pennsauken, New Jersey**

**Pittsburg, Kansas**

**Darlington, South Carolina**

Darlington, South Carolina, holds a festival each Labor Day. The festival began in 1950, when the first Southern 500 stock car race was held. Today, thousands of people attend the race.

**Morgan City, Louisiana**

Seafood workers in Morgan City, Louisiana, held their first street parade on Labor Day in 1936. The event, which also honors oil workers, has grown into a four-day celebration called the Louisiana Shrimp and Petroleum Festival. Special events include the crowning of a festival king and queen, water and street parades, and cooking contests.

# Holiday Symbols

Many symbols such as statues and monuments are found across the United States. These symbols remind people of the efforts of workers and labor activists. Symbols can teach people about current labor issues, too. The following symbols honor workers and labor activists.

## American Labor Museum

In 1913, more than 20,000 silk mill workers went on strike. Labor leaders spoke to thousands of strikers from the home of **immigrant** mill worker Pietro Botto and his wife Maria. Their home, in Haledon, New Jersey, is now known as the Botto House. It is also the American Labor Museum.

The museum has a library and rooms that depict how workers and immigrants lived in the early 1900s. The museum also has educational programs and tours.

★ ★ ★ ★ ★ ★ ★ ★ ★ ★

The American Labor Museum holds a Labor Day celebration each year.

## Postage Stamps

Many special stamps have been made by the United States Postal Service to honor workers and labor leaders. In 1950, a stamp was made to honor Samuel Gompers. In 1956, a special Labor Day stamp was created. A picture of Frances Perkins, the first female Secretary of Labor, was put on a stamp in 1980. In 1998, a Child Labor Reform stamp was made to raise awareness of child labor conditions around the world.

## The Labor Hall of Fame

Each year a ceremony is held at the U.S. Department of Labor in Washington, D.C. This celebration honors American citizens who have helped improve working conditions and workers' rights. A display is set up in the Hall of Fame to honor these people. The display includes a portrait of each person and a video. In 2002, the display honored the rescue workers who helped people trapped inside the Pentagon and the World Trade Center on September 11, 2001.

# Further Research

Many books and Web sites have information about the history and traditions of Labor Day. These Web sites and books can help you learn more.

## Web Sites

To find out more about the U.S. Department of Labor, visit:
**www.dol.gov**

To learn about labor symbols, visit:
**www.laborheritage.org**

To explore the AFL-CIO, visit:
**www.aflcio.org**

## Books

Carey, Charles W. *Eugene V. Debs: Outspoken Labor Leader and Socialist.* New Jersey: Enslow Publishers, Inc., 2003.

Saller, Carol. *Working Children.* Minnesota: Carolrhoda Books, 2003.

# Crafts and Recipes

## Collage of Workers

There are many fun projects you can create for Labor Day. For example, you can make a Labor Day collage by cutting pictures of workers out of magazines and gluing them onto a poster board. You will need old magazines, scissors, glue, poster board, and markers. First, cut out a variety of pictures of workers, such as doctors, painters, and police officers. Then, glue the pictures on the poster board. Use the markers to decorate the collage.

## Be a Town Planner

Create a town using a piece of poster board and crayons. Think about the types of buildings, stores, and offices your town will need, such as a gas station, grocery store, hospital, and school. Draw your town on the poster board. Make a list of the types of workers you will need to run these buildings, such as cashiers, doctors, and teachers. Write which jobs are available beneath each building.

# Labor Day Recipe

## Make a Perfect Potato Salad

**Ingredients:**

2 pounds of peeled, red potatoes

1/3 cup sliced celery

1/3 cup chopped onion

1/3 cup grated carrots

1 1/2 tbsp sweet pickle relish

1/3 cup mayonnaise

1/3 cup sour cream

2 tbsp spicy mustard

1/4 tsp ground black pepper

**Equipment:**

large bowl

small bowl

knife

salad tosser

1. With an adult's help, cut the potatoes into 3/4-inch pieces.
2. Cover the potatoes, and cook them in a microwave for 8 to 10 minutes.
3. Rinse the potatoes with cool water, and drain.
4. Place the potatoes in the large bowl along with the carrots, celery, onion, and relish. Gently toss the mixture with the salad tosser.
5. Combine the mayonnaise, sour cream, spicy mustard, and ground black pepper in the small bowl.
6. Add the contents of the small bowl to the potato mixture, and gently toss.
7. Cover the salad, and chill for at least 2 hours.

# Holiday Quiz

What have you learned about Labor Day? See if you can answer the following questions. Check your answers on the next page.

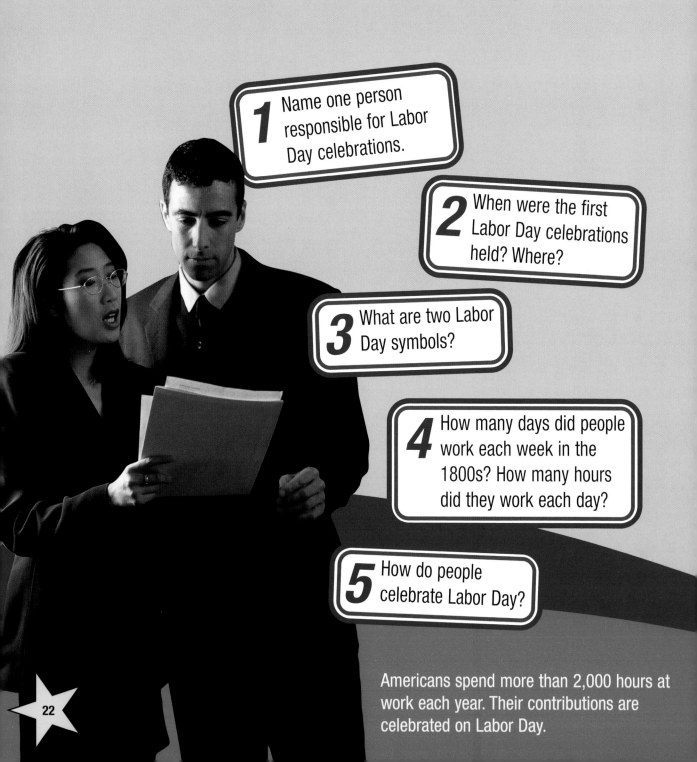

**1** Name one person responsible for Labor Day celebrations.

**2** When were the first Labor Day celebrations held? Where?

**3** What are two Labor Day symbols?

**4** How many days did people work each week in the 1800s? How many hours did they work each day?

**5** How do people celebrate Labor Day?

Americans spend more than 2,000 hours at work each year. Their contributions are celebrated on Labor Day.

# Fascinating Facts

★ The U.S. Department of Labor was created in 1913. One of their goals is to protect and improve working conditions.

★ Books and movies tell about workers' challenges. The movie *Newsies* is about an 1899 newspaper boys' strike in New York City. The book *Lyddie*, by Katherine Paterson, is about one girl's experiences working in a textile mill in the 1840s.

★ A statue in Auburn, California, honors Chinese workers who helped build the railroad.

★ In 1938, U.S. Congress passed the Fair Labor Standards Act. This act includes better **child labor laws**. For example, no one under the age of 14 can work at a job.

**Quiz Answers:**
1. Peter J. McGuire or Matthew Maguire
2. The first Labor Day celebrations were held on September 5, 1882, in New York City.
3. The American Labor Museum, postage stamps, or The Labor Hall of Fame
4. People worked 6 or 7 days each week. They worked 10 to 14 hours each day.
5. People celebrate Labor Day by relaxing with family and friends, attending sporting events, and visiting beaches, parks, or campgrounds. Some communities hold parades and festivals on Labor Day.

# Glossary

**activists:** people who take action and make their ideas about an issue known

**child labor laws:** federal and state rules that protect young workers

**comedian:** a person who makes people laugh by telling jokes

**craftspeople:** people who are skilled at a certain type of work

**immigrant:** a person who comes to live in another country

**labor union:** a group of workers who join together to protect or gain worker rights

**monument:** something built in memory of a person or event

**protests:** gatherings where people express their unhappiness toward something

**strikes:** protests during which workers stop working

**trade:** work that requires a special skill

# Index